Tales from the Tao

tales from the Tao

Inspirational Teachings
from the Great Taoist Masters

Solala Towler

photographs by
John Cleare

WATKINS
LONDON

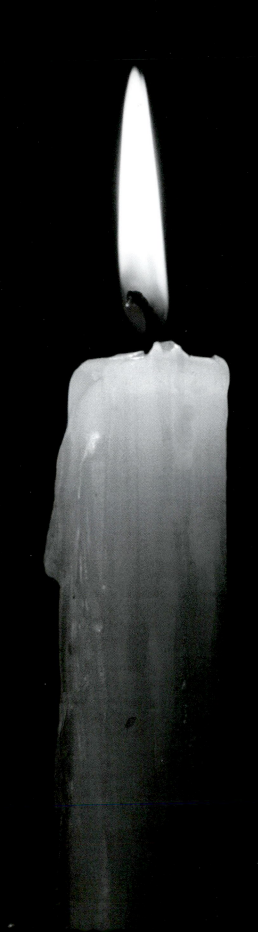

This edition published in
the UK in 2005 by
Watkins Publishing
Sixth Floor, Castle House
75-76 Wells Street
London W1T 3QH

Designed and typeset by
Jerry Goldie Gaphic Design

Printed and bound in
Thailand

British Library Cataloguing in
Publication data available

Library of Congress
Cataloguing in Publication
data available

ISBN 1 84293 130 X

www.watkinspublishing.com

Contents

Abode of the Eternal Tao

Year of the Yin Wood Phoenix

The Tales

Tale 1

We Shall See

There was once an old man who had one son and one horse, both of whom he valued very highly. One day the horse ran away and his neighbors came over to console him. 'Oh what great misfortune,' they said, 'your horse is gone! How will you ever afford to get another?'

The old man sat and smoked his pipe and only said, 'We shall see.'

Then, a few days later, the horse came back, accompanied by several wild horses, tripling his herd. Again the neighbors visited, this time to congratulate the old man on his great luck. Again he merely sat and smoked and said, 'We shall see.'

A short time later, his son was thrown from one of the wild horses and broke his leg in several places. The neighbors all arrived, calling out, 'Ah great misfortune, your son will never walk again!' But again the old man merely sat quietly in front of his house and, between puffs of his pipe, said, 'We shall see.'

Some time after that, the army came though the village, rounding up all the young men to press them into service and send them to the battlefront far away in the frozen north. But with his crippled leg the old man's son was left behind. Though crippled, he managed to care for his old father until his death many years later.

LIEH TZU

What is right in one case is not what is

   right in another;

What is wrong in one case is not what

   is wrong in another.

HUAINANZI

In the world of knowledge,

Every day something new is added.

In pursuit of the Tao,

Every day something is let go.

LAO TZU

Tale 2

To Be or Not to Be, A Butterfly

The butterfly flitted on its way, unmindful of the gentle breeze that ruffled its wings. It flew here and there, content in its own way to wander without a goal, without any needs except to be part of the breeze that blew past its wings as it flew along, unhurried, unfurled and even.

This little butterfly's life had been brief. From caterpillar to chrysalis inside its quiet and heavy cocoon, it had stayed for what seemed eons of time - quiet, patient, waiting for the moment when it could break out of its prison, unfurl its wings and fly straight up into the air.

Now it did just so, flitting around in circles, occasionally meeting up with another butterfly, always mindful of predators or a strong and sudden gust of wind that could tear at its thin, translucent wings and send it hurtling down to earth.

Now and again the butterfly seemed to have glimpses of another life, another form. It seemed to be a much heavier and more ponderous life, this other one. But usually the butterfly ignored these unsettling inner sightings and just did what butterflies do, without thought, without motive, without any other goal than just to be what it was, a butterfly flying free.

And as it did so the day lengthened into night and the butterfly headed back to the tree where it slept through the long period of darkness. It flew gently towards it and then suddenly stopped.

The man lay in his bed, bewildered, bemused, lost in thought. It had seemed so real to him, this gentle butterfly life. He lay in the early morning light, listening to the sounds of the village as it slowly came to wake all about him. He heard the creaking of doors as people made their way to the outhouses. He heard the sudden squall of an infant, the bark of a dog, the clomp of an ox as it trudged out to the fields, led by its sleepy master. He heard the sounds of fires being built, the tea kettles and the rice pots being readied for breakfast.

He lay there a long time, without rising, without moving, other than the slow and deep rising and falling of his belly as he breathed his way into the day. His dream, if that is what it was, had been so vivid,

so real. He had actually experienced himself as that butterfly - had felt the breeze on his wings, felt himself carried through the air as light as a seed, had thought only butterfly thoughts.

Yet now, here he was, back in his human body, back in the world of cause and effect. But which was truly real and which was the dream - himself as a butterfly, or himself as a man, waiting here for his students to come and drag him out into the light of day with their incessant questions and demands?

How did he know that what he was experiencing now was not the dream? That he really was that butterfly, living its simple butterfly life, unattached and a part of the great natural world of Tao. He smiled in the darkness then. Truly, it did not matter if he was a man who had dreamed he was a butterfly or a butterfly who was now dreaming he was a man. He knew what he knew and he knew what he didn't know. That was what sustained him through the long days and nights of his human life. What he knew or experienced in his butterfly life was also there, just outside the periphery of his vision.

He almost laughed out loud. Imagine if I shared this with my students, he thought. He could just see their faces as he explained to them that he was not truly sure if what he experienced in his human life was any more real than what he experienced in his butterfly life.

He slowly rose from his bed, and, stretching out his arms above him like the slow unfolding of butterfly wings, went forth into the day.

CHUANG TZU

The space between heaven and earth is
   like a bellows.

It is empty yet never loses its form.

It moves yet keeps on moving.

Many words are not as good as a few.

Maintain the center.

LAO TZU

The Horse Breeder

Pen Lo had bred horses for the duke for many years. Now he was getting old and the duke asked him if there was anyone in his family who would be able to take over from him.

Pen Lo said, 'You can tell a good horse by looking at its muscles and appearance, but the best horses are the ones that cannot be judged by their appearance only. You must be able to see their inner nature. No one in my family has this ability, but I do know of one man who might be able to help you. He is a poor man who hauls wood and vegetables for a living yet he has the ability to differentiate the superior horse from the merely great.'

The duke was happy then and sent for the man and asked him to find him a special horse. The man was gone for three months and then sent word to the duke that he had found such a horse.

'What kind of horse is it?' asked the duke.

'It is a yellow mare,' came the answer.

So the duke sent for the horse and it turned out to be a black stallion. He was angry then and sent for Pen Lo. 'This man you sent to me knows nothing about horses,' he said. 'He cannot even tell a mare from a stallion, never mind yellow from black.'

Pen Lo's face lit up. 'Ah,' he said, 'It is even better than I had hoped. His ability is now ten thousand times greater than mine. He has completely transcended judging a horse by its appearance and sees only its inner nature. When he looks at the horse he does not see a male or female or what color it is but looks instead to its very essence. In this way he can see the potential for greatness in a horse.'

Indeed, when he had sent for the horse, the duke found that it was the greatest horse he had ever seen.

LIEH TZU

Hold the body and spirit as one.

Can you avoid their separation?

Concentrating your chi and becoming
   pliant,

Can you become like a newborn baby?

Clearing your mind and contemplating
   the profound,

Can you remain unflawed?

LAO TZU

The two messengers, who wore costly robes of silk, were struggling to hold up their hems to avoid getting them muddied. They were out of breath by the time they reached the old man, who sat with his back to them.

'Honored sir,' they panted. 'Are you the one they call ...?' They used an honorific title he had been given years ago at the capital in recognition of his sagehood. He thought at first of denying it but realized they already knew who he was when they first climbed down the riverbank. They were only using a formality. He knew it all so well - the empty, flowery phrases that fell from their tongues like rancid butter.

Sighing, he got up slowly and turned to face them. 'Yes,' he answered. 'I am that most unworthy person.' He knew how to play the game.

The two silken messengers looked at each other. Could this really be the great sage that their lord had sent them after? Why, he looked like a ragged fisherman! Yet there was something about his direct and piercing gaze that held them for a moment, like the sun coming out from behind a cloud. Then, just as suddenly, it was gone again and the old man stood before them, idly picking his nose.
'We have been sent by the great lord of this province to bid you come to his castle so he may humbly prostrate himself before you and beg of you to share some small part of your great wisdom with his lowly household.'

What rubbish! The old man knew just what would happen if he allowed himself to be led to the castle. Hours and hours of fawning and false modesty, to be followed by days and days of being a virtual prisoner, arguing with a dimwitted nobleman who had never had an original thought in his head. He would have to deal with whatever other 'sages' the noble had ensconced there to argue philosophy before him. All his life he had dealt with those high-minded, long-winded Confucians who confused propriety and wisdom, duty and Tao, classism and true spiritual freedom. He wanted no more to do with them.

And the logicians were even worse. How they loved to confuse and conspire with endless torrents of words - words with no spirit or real energy behind them, words which clouded one's thoughts and induced a narcotic, hypnotic effect that numbed the mind to the true reality of the Way. How many endless hours had he already spent trying to get them to let go of their precious concepts and opinions and open themselves to the simple, unadorned truth of the integral and eternal Way?

No, he could not stomach any more of that. He had to find a way to turn them away without incurring the wrath of their great lord. Suddenly an idea came to him. 'You have the shell of a ritual tortoise at the castle, do you not?'

The two messengers did not know what to say. This old man was a little abrupt. They had expected him to jump at the chance to be set up in the castle. After all, he would be paid well for his efforts and he would be wearing much finer clothing than the old rags he presently wore and be enveloped in much richer surroundings than this mosquito-infested, muddy riverbank.

'Yes,' answered one of them finally, 'we do have a great and ancient tortoise shell which, as you most assuredly know, great sage, is used for divination at certain times of the year.'

The old man could imagine the pomp and circumstance of the divination ceremony: the ancient tortoise shell would be carried into the hall of divination between rows and rows of seated nobles and servants, all stiff and formal. The procession would be accompanied by the ancient sing-song music of the Confucians, more irritating and less musical than the whining of the mosquitoes in his ear. Endless speeches and formal testimonials would follow. At last would come the ceremonial heating of the tortoise shell; the cracks that appeared on it could then be read. Would the year in question be good or bad for the great lord and his fief? The priests were not fools; they were not stupid enough to share bad tidings, even if they read them on the tortoise shell. The great lord would not want to know about the floods, the

many farmers going hungry, the diseases and the pestilence that would be visited upon the common people that year. No, he would want to hear how beneficent and wise he was, what a great ruler of men he was, what a generous and compassionate father to his people he was. The very thought of it made the old man want to vomit right there at the silken feet of the great lord's messengers.

'Well,' he said, 'what do you fellows think? I can see you are intelligent men. If the tortoise himself had been given the choice between being slaughtered for his shell to be venerated for hundreds of years or to be left alone to drag his tail in the mud, what do you think the tortoise would have wanted?'

The two messengers looked at each other again. Was this some kind of test? They had been told that the old man was a bit odd, some even thought him crazy. They both decided to take their time in answering, just in case. Finally one of them took a deep breath and spoke. 'I suppose,' he said slowly, 'that if it were truly up to the tortoise, why of course he would rather have been left alone to, as you say, drag his tail through the mud.'

'Then that is precisely what I intend to do with mine,' said the old man and abruptly turned his back on them, his muddy bottom winking obscenely. He gathered up his fishing line and trudged down the bank, singing an old folk song at the top of his lungs.

The messengers watched him for some time as he walked slowly away. What would they say to the great lord? They were not even sure themselves what had just happened. To think they had walked all this way and gotten muddy and mosquito bitten for this! It was true, they would tell their lord, the old man was crazy, not a sage, not a wise man. Just a crazy old man sitting on his bottom in the mud.

CHUANG TZU

Do not seek fame. Do not make plans.
Do not be absorbed by activities. Do
not think that you know. Be aware of
all that is and dwell in the infinite.
Wander where there is no path. Be all
that heaven gave you, but act as
though you have received nothing.
Be empty, that is all.

CHUANG TZU

The ancient achieved ones
were masters at penetrating the subtle
and profound Tao.

They were so deep that we cannot
describe them.

They were cautious, like someone
fording a frozen river.

They were vigilant, like someone who is
surrounded by enemies.

They were courteous, like dignified guests.

They were ephemeral, like melting ice.

They were simple, like the uncarved block.

They were open and wide, like a valley.

They were deep, like swirling water.

LAO TZU

A Calm Awakening

Tzu Lai lay dying, surrounded by his wife and children, who were all weeping. His friend Tzu Li came to see him and finding them thus, said to the family, 'Be quiet, do not disturb him in his time of great transformation!' Then he spoke to his friend saying, 'Great is the creator of life. What will he make you in your next life do you think - the liver of a rat, or a bug's leg?'

Tzu Lai smiled and answered, 'The relationship of a child to his parents is that he follows their directions, no matter where they lead. The relationship of yin and yang are even more important than that. If they urge me to die now, I must humbly submit, otherwise I am being obstinate and rebellious. The great earth gives me a form, I toil on it, in my old age I find my ease on it, and at death I am able to rest in it. That which makes my life good also makes my death good.'

It is said that we are born from a quiet sleep and that at death, we slip into a calm awakening.

CHUANG TZU

36

When your work is done, withdraw,

This is the Way of Heaven.

LAO TZU

People follow the way
of Earth;

Earth follows the way
of Heaven;

Heaven follows the
way of Tao;

Tao follows its own
natural way.

LAO TZU

Tale 6

The Value of Worthlessness

A certain carpenter was traveling with his helper. They came to a town where a giant oak tree filled the square. It was huge, with many limbs spreading out; large enough to shade a hundred oxen and its shade covered the entire square. The helper was amazed at the potential lumber contained in this one tree but the carpenter passed it by with a mere glance. When his helper asked him why he had passed up such a magnificent specimen the carpenter replied that he could see at once that the great oak's branches were useless to him.

'They are so hard,' he said, 'that were I to take my ax to them it would split. The wood is so heavy that a boat made of it would sink. The branches themselves are so gnarled and twisted they cannot be made into planks. If I tried to fashion house beams with it they would collapse. If I made a coffin from it you would not be able to fit someone inside. Altogether it is a completely useless tree. And that is the secret of its long life.'

CHUANG TZU

The trees on the mountain can be used
 to build and so are cut down.

When fat is added to the fire it
 consumes itself.

Cinnamon can be eaten and so is
 harvested.

The lacquer tree can be used and so is
 slashed.

Everyone knows the usefulness of the
 useful

But no one knows the usefulness of the
 useless!

CHUANG TZU

42

Dreaming of Gold

There once lived a man in Chi who was obsessed with gold. But he was so poor that he was never able to amass more than one gold coin, old and shabby and clipped about the sides. This man arose from his bed each morning thinking about gold and then went to bed at night to dream about it. But no matter how hard he tried he could never earn any more gold. He went around to every rich man's house and asked for work. But the only work that he was given was menial and extremely badly paid. He tried to gamble with the rough men outside the wine shop but lost almost every time, until he had lost even his one shabby piece of gold.

One day he got up at dawn, got dressed and set out for the marketplace. He went over to the stall that dealt in gold, snatched up a great gold bar and ran off down the street. In his haste to get away he ran right into the constable and was dragged off to prison.

At his arraignment the judge asked him, 'What did you think you were doing stealing someone else's gold right in front of so many people?'

'When I took the gold,' he replied, 'I did not see any other people. I only saw the gold.'

Thus do we all often lose sight of what is really precious in our lives by only concentrating on what we wish were so instead of what is.

Lieh Tzu

Something mysteriously formed,

Born before heaven and earth.

In the silence and the void,

Standing alone and unchanging,

Ever present and in motion.

Perhaps it is the Mother of the Ten
    Thousand Things.

I do not know its name.

So I call it Tao.

LAO TZU

But the shaman would not stop. Soon after that he disappeared from his mountain home and was never seen in those parts again.

When Lieh Tzu asked his master what had happened Hu Tzu told him, 'I merely showed him my true self, before I came into being - like grass bending before the wind on the steppes and as water flowing in waves across a vast sea. I opened myself completely to him and he was frightened by what he saw and ran away.'

Lieh Tzu saw then that his master was indeed a true man of Tao. Tearfully, he bade Hu Tzu goodbye and went back to his home, where he lived for three years without going out into the world. He let his wife rest and did all the cooking and he fed the pigs as if they were people and old friends. He took no part in the goings on of the world but kept himself whole and plain, like a block of wood or clump of earth.

And slowly, little by little, he began to understand what his teacher had been trying to tell him all those years. He gave up trying to learn everything. He gave up trying to be good. He gave up trying to become enlightened. He began to experience himself as one with the great unending Tao and he remained close to the Tao until the end of his days.

LIEH TZU

'When the ocean of internal *chi* is disturbed, it makes waves swirl to a great depth. There are nine levels to this depth. I have nine centers of *chi* in my body, three of which I showed to him, which confused his poor stupid head. Bring him back to me one more time.'

This time Lieh Tzu stood very near the door so that he could hear what was going on inside. But no sooner had the shaman gone into Hu Tzu's house when he came running back out again, necklaces clanking, with a wild and terrified look on this face, knocking Lieh Tzu to the ground. 'Wait,' cried Lieh Tzu, 'what happened?'

my *yuan chi*, my primordial energy, welling up from my heels. Doubtless that is what he saw as a good sign. Bring him before me again.'

So the next day the shaman came again. This time when he left Hu Tzu's house he was shaking his head. 'I do not understand,' he said. 'This master of yours is never the same for one day. The day before yesterday I saw death in his face, yesterday it seemed to me that I saw life. Today I am confused. I cannot read his face at all. Let his spirit settle down first, then I will be able to read him clearly.' And again, he strode off, still shaking his head.

Lieh Tzu went in to see his teacher, who greeted him with a smile. 'I just showed him the Tai Chi, the Great Ultimate,' he said, 'where all primal qualities are in perfect balance and harmony. Of course all the ignorant oaf saw was the perfect balance of my internal *chi*.

The Shaman and the Taoist

Long ago, in the state of Cheng, there lived a powerful shaman. This shaman had many spirit helpers and could read any man or woman's destiny just by looking at their face. He could tell them about their past and future, gain and loss, fortune and misfortune. He could also tell anyone the exact time of their death - including year, month, day and even hour.

Of course he was feared by many people, who usually passed him with their faces averted. After all, it is only the most brave or foolish who wish to know such dire news. When he would come into the village from his mountain home, with his long matted hair, clothed in rags and furs, with many amulets of bones, stones, and animal parts all clanking about him, his eyes blazing with a fierce and animal-like fire, people would flee.

Lieh Tzu, the young student of the Taoist master Hu Tzu, and a very inquisitive sort, decided that he needed to meet such a powerful and feared man and so went up the mountain to visit him. He entered the shaman's hut and, after allowing a few moments for his eyes to adjust to the gloom of the smoke-filled room, sat himself down before the shaman.

The shaman looked back at the young man with a fierce, almost savage look. He shook one of his ox-hide rattles at him and asked what he wanted. Did he want his fortune told? Did he want to know the year, month, day and hour of his death?

The sage practices non-action.

She teaches by not speaking,

Achieves in all things while
undertaking nothing,

Creates but does not take
credit,

Acts but does not depend,

Accomplishes much while not
claiming merit.

Because she claims no merit,

Her work will last forever.

LAO TZU

Tale 9

The Fortunate Hunchback

There was once a hunchbacked man named Shu. He was so deformed his chin rested on his navel, his shoulders rose up over his head, his topknot pointed to the sky, his organs were all squashed together and his thigh bones were in line with his hips. But by washing clothes and sewing he was able to support himself.

He also winnowed and sifted grain and, in this way, was able to make enough to support ten people. When soldiers came to the village to press men into the emperor's armies, Shu was always passed over. When work gangs were formed to build great public projects, Shu was exempt. And lastly, when the government gave out wood and grain to the needy, he always got more than anyone!

If this poor man was able to support himself so ably, how much easier it should be for those of us whose deformities are those of the mind!

CHUANG TZU

If one is true to one's self and follows
its teaching, who need be without a
teacher?

CHUANG TZU

Be careful of your words,

For someone will agree with
  them.

Be careful of your conduct,

For someone will imitate it.

LIEH TZU

Tale 10

To Dream the Impossible Dream

grim and obsessive, in the general
onrush of the human herd, unable to
stop themselves or to change their
direction. All the while they claim to
be just on the point of attaining
happiness. My opinion is that you
never find happiness until you stop
looking for it.

CHUANG TZU

Dancing the Yin/Yang

Once upon a time an old man and a young boy journeyed together up a mountain. The boy was full of innocence and impatience and the old man was filled with experience and quietude. The boy was at the beginning of a great adventure. The old man was near the end of a long and arduous journey, one that he had begun many years before and that had been filled to overflowing with experiences that he would never have been able to describe to another. The boy was restless and wandering; every little butterfly sent him chasing perilously close to the cliff's edge. The old man was solid and resigned, yet still amused and entertained by the boy's reckless abandon.

As they reached the top of the mountain they met an old woman and a young girl climbing up from the other side. They shared the common characteristics of the boy and the old man. The girl was young and full of youthful vigor and vitality. The old woman was wise and serene, yet still able to smile easily and laugh heartily. They too had been on a long and at times perilous journey and they too were now at the end of their quest.

Upon reaching the summit of the mountain the old man, young boy, old woman, and young girl all sat down to rest together in the shade of an ancient and gnarled oak tree. They sat together and looked out over the valley spread before them like a painting from the Tang dynasty. The old woman looked over at the young girl and smiled and the old man look over at the young man and grinned. Then they nodded to each other. Words were not needed and so none were offered. Instead they all sat there, lost in time, floating in space, while the great birds wheeled overhead and the mountain breezes played with their long hair.

Then, after a long time - hours, years, eons - they all turned to each other and, after standing, bowed deeply to each other. Then, like a living yin/yang symbol, they began to dance in flowing circles around and within each other. On and on they danced while the sun slid slowly down over the horizon, then on into the night, under the crystalline star blanket. After a time they began to merge into each other until at last there remained only the faintest trace of their presence. A great circle, with two entwined fish-like semicircles remained, each giving birth and finding completion in the other. The spiritual remains of the old man and the old woman still flowed endlessly out of and into each other and the youthful energy of the young boy and the young girl remained there, spinning within the circle of the old man and old woman.

To this day, certain climbers and hikers - those with clear vision and deep insight - have reported a strange and wonderful sight on top of that mountain. Some people say that they have had visions of four people dancing together in a circle, endlessly flowing and melting into each other. Others swear they hear the sounds of laughter and music in the air, coming from somewhere just above their heads. Others feel they have sensed a presence of joy, wisdom, and deep compassion emanating from the very rocks and trees on that mountaintop.

Other people, of course, have seen, heard, and felt nothing - only the quiet sound of the wind blowing across the mountain. These are people who dare not dream in the day and do not sleep deeply in the night. They do not fly on the wings of imagination nor flow with the energy of the universe as it courses through their own bodies. They are, of course, in the majority.

Yet, those who do see, hear, and feel the living yin/yang symbol there on the mountaintop are never quite the same.

SOLALA TOWLER

The Tao is an empty vessel;

it is used but never

exhausted.

It is the fathomless source

of the ten thousand things!

LAO TZU

Tale 12

Showing Off

It was a high, bright day and Lieh Tzu was showing off his mastery of archery. He had a bowl of water placed on his left forearm after he had drawn his bow. After releasing his first arrow he quickly fitted another and then another, releasing each arrow while the one before it was still in flight. All the while the bowl of water did not spill a drop.

His master, observing him, asked, 'If we climbed a high mountain pass and stood on the edge of a cliff overlooking an abyss of a thousand feet deep, would you still be able to shoot like this?'

'Of course,' said Lieh Tzu. 'I have practiced shooting from my horse as well as hitting a moving target. As a master of the bow I am sure that shooting from a cliff will be no problem.'

83

So off they went together up to the top of the mountain. His master walked backwards to the edge of the cliff and stood with half of one foot hung over the edge and bade Lieh Tzu to come forward. When Lieh Tzu reached the edge of the cliff and looked over the edge into the bottomless abysss he felt himself grow dizzy and had to lie down.

His face was drenched in sweat and his hands were shaking so badly he was not able to hold his bow.

His master laughed and said, 'The true master can shoot an arrow under any condition. Whether he is looking into the blue sky above him or the abyss of death below him he is not affected. Nothing can damage his peace of mind. Look at you. You are shaking so badly you can't even hold your bow. How can you call yourself a master?'

LIEH TZU

Those who are good at walking

leave no tracks;

Those who are good at

speaking make no mistakes;

Those who are good at

calculating need no counters;

Those who are good at closing

things need no key,

Yet what they close cannot be

opened.

LAO TZU

Hearing of an Immortal

A student named Chien Wu came to his master Lien Shu and said, 'I heard Chieh Yu speaking yesterday and his words upset me. They seemed to have nothing to do with reality. They seemed to me like the stars in the Milky Way, far away and unattainable. They confused and even frightened me.'

'What did he say?' asked Lien Shu.

'He said that far away, on Ku Mountain there lives an immortal whose flesh and skin are as white and smooth as snow. He is as fine and delicate as a young girl. It is said that he never eats food but subsides on air and dew. He mounts the clouds and rides on the back of dragons, wandering all about the four seas. With his spirit powers he can protect anyone from sickness or decay and ensure a bountiful harvest. This seems to me to be ridiculous and I cannot believe any of it.'

Lien Shu then told him, 'Everything Chieh Yu says is true. The blind cannot see elegant shapes and the deaf cannot hear the music of the

bells and drums. But blindness and deafness are not just physical, they can also be mental. So it is with yourself. This immortal looks upon all the different manifestations of the world as one. Because of him, we are all better for it. Nothing can harm such a person. A great flood could not drown him. The greatest heat, one that could melt metals and stone, could not harm him. From his very being he could fashion great philosopher kings. Why should he bother with our world?'

CHUANG TZU

The Tao that can be put into words

is not the true and eternal Tao.

LAO TZU

Tale 14

A Tale of Two Lovers

Long ago there was a young man named Wang Chou who was in love with a young woman named Ch'ien Niang. They had grown up together and had often pictured each other in their secret dreams. But their love remained a secret and so, when Ch'ien Niang came of marriageable age, her father decided to wed her to one of his staff.

Wang Chou was heartbroken. He decided to go to the far off capital where he wouldn't have to see his love with another man. And so he trudged off into the countryside, shoulders slumped, tears filling his eyes.

That night, as slept along the river, he was awakened by the sound of footsteps and then he heard someone breathing right next to him. At first he thought it was a bandit and so steeled himself for a fight. But, to his surprise, it was Ch'ien Niang, who had run away to be with him. So they went off together, quickly and quietly and traveled as far as they were able, helped by some friendly boatmen.

They went as far away as they could and then settled down. Wang Chou was able to find work as a boatman and the years passed. They had two sons and were very happy. But Ch'ien Niang felt guilty about how she had left her family and yearned to see them again. Finally, after years had passed, they decided it would be safe to visit her family and so they went back to their village.

When they arrived Wang Chou went to Ch'ien Niang's home first, just in case everyone was still angry. When he tried to apologize for Ch'ien Niang's unfilial behavior, however, her father said that Ch'ien Niang was there, lying in her room, where she had been ill for all those years.

'But she is back in the boat with her two children,' said Wang Chou. Her father did not believe him and so sent a servant down to the boat to see if it were true. When the servant reported back that Ch'ien Niang was indeed on the boat, the sick girl rose from her bed, put on her jewelry and finest clothes and went forth to greet the woman from the boat.

When Ch'ien Niang saw her double walking toward her she almost fainted. But behind her she could see her parents, who were looking at her with a look of surprise and even a little fear. The two Ch'ien Niangs continued to walk toward each other until they met. It is said that when they did, their two bodies merged, each with the other and, to everyone's amazement, they became one, fitting together perfectly. It was then that everyone noticed that, although there was only one woman now, she was wearing two sets of clothing!

CH'EN HSUAN-YU

94

Without going out your door,

You can know the whole world.

Without looking through your window,

You can see the Tao of Heaven.

LAO TZU

'Crazy' Tuan-mu Shu

Tuan-mu Shu had inherited his family fortune, said to be worth ten thousand pieces of gold. He never had to work and lived in a fabulous mansion surrounded with gardens, lakes, terraces, and pavilions. His food and clothing, as well as that of his various wives and concubines, were of the finest quality. He went wherever he wished, traveling far and wide, collecting treasures and exploring anything that he became interested in.

Every day he had hundreds of guests, and it was said that the fires in his kitchen were never allowed to go out. He and his guests were entertained by the finest musicians and dancers in the land. The leftovers of his banquets were distributed far and wide and his generosity to anyone in need was legendary.

Then, when he reached the age of sixty, he suddenly changed his life completely. He gave away all of his wealth and possessions, not even saving some for his wives and children. Finally he became ill and was too poor to pay for the doctor and so he died. His children had no money to pay for a funeral but the townspeople, remembering his generosity to them over the years, took up a collection. This was more than enough to pay for his funeral, with sufficient left over to give to his family.

A prominent Confucian heard about this and he called Tuan-mu Shu a madman, and said he had disgraced his ancestors. When the Taoist master heard about it he laughed and called Tuan-mu Shu enlightened. 'This man was in touch with his essential self,' he said. 'He lived by his own spirit and never did anything that went against his true nature. He spent his money when he had it and then gave it away when he no longer needed it. Some may say he was crazy for abandoning his wealth and even the wealth of his family but all he did was follow his own heart, without any constraints or worries about the future. His mind was of such a subtle nature that most people could never understand him.'

LIEH TZU

99

Stop filling when the vessel is full.

A knife sharpened too often will not
   retain its edge.

If gold and jade fill your home it will be
   impossible to defend.

Arrogant wealth and rank will bring its
   own punishment.

Withdraw after good deeds,

This is the Way of Tao.

LAO TZU

Tale *16*

On Eating

A teacher was traveling with some of her students. At one of their stops they were served the meat of a pig. The students were horrified to see the teacher calmly eating this forbidden food. 'Teacher,' they cried, 'is not the flesh of an animal forbidden by our order?'

The teacher went on chewing slowly, clearly savoring the taste of the pig. When she had finished she said, 'Can you not see that it was a great and honored gift from these poor people to be given this delicacy? No doubt it was given at great cost to them and with an attitude of humbleness and generosity. Who am I to spurn their gift?

'Besides,' she said, taking another bite, 'it is not what goes into your mouth that defiles you, but what comes out.'

SOLALA TOWLER

102

Under heaven nothing is more soft and
weaker than water.

Yet for attacking the hard, the resistant,
nothing can surpass it.

The weak can conquer the strong,

The soft can conquer the hard.

Under heaven everyone knows this

Yet no one seems to apply it.

LAO TZU

The Emperor and the Sage

Things had been going from bad to worse. It seemed that no matter how the emperor ruled, things turned out badly. There had been famines and wars throughout the land. There was even conflict within the august household itself. The emperor's many wives quarreled amongst themselves continually and even his advisors stood in the great hall, shaking their ancient heads and pulling on their equally

ancient beards. It had begun to be whispered in the marketplace and in the fields of the laborers that the emperor had lost heaven's favor and so would soon lose his place on the dragon throne. For, as everyone knew, once a ruler loses heaven's favor, it would not be long before he would be overthrown.

His advisors seemed to be of no help whatsoever. In truth, all they ever wanted was to advance themselves in his favor and would tell him only what they thought he wanted to hear. When he was young he enjoyed this but as he became older and more interested in being a good ruler, he found himself becoming impatient with the lackeys and sycophants around him.

He had spent many nights locked in with his astrologers, who had assured him that he had been born under a lucky star and could do no wrong. Then he had spent further nights with the experts on the *Book of Changes,* only to be told that all hexagrams pointed to great success and longevity for his dynasty.

But he knew something was wrong and that he would get no honest answers at court and so he decided to travel to the mountains to visit a certain Taoist sage who lived high on the craggy top. It was said that the sage lived on moonlight and dew and knew the future of any man that came before him. He was sure, or course, that this was all nonsense, but he decided it would not hurt to try.

For many days he traveled, with a large escort in case of bandits. He enjoyed sleeping under the stars at night, which he had not done since he was a boy. He also enjoyed beginning each day's journey in the brisk bright air of the morning. His usually poor appetite improved and he even put on a little weight.

Finally they reached the path that led to the cave where it was said that the sage resided. The emperor decided to go on alone, ordering his personal guards to stay behind, much to their dismay.

When he reached the cave he found it abandoned, and felt bereft and sad that he had missed the one man who could assist him. On the way down from the cave he ran into an old man sitting by the side of the path, combing his fingers through his long beard and humming to himself.

This must be the sage, he thought to himself, and though he was the emperor and ruler of all under heaven, he knelt before the old man and beseeched him to give some advice on how best to rule the country.

The old man seemed to ignore the emperor for some time and the emperor began to wonder if this was indeed the man he had been looking for. With his mind in turmoil, the emperor began to make ready to leave this addled old man and give up on his quest for the sage when he suddenly noticed that, though the old man seemed to be sitting on a stone on the side of the path he was actually floating, a few inches only, just above the ground. Then he knew that he had indeed found the sage that he had been looking for, and began to plead with him for advice on how to rule his vast country.

'I have knowledge only about ruling my own life,' said the sage. 'I don't know anything about ruling a country.' He then went back to humming and combing his beard, which though thin, was extremely long.

'But I have a responsibility to manage the shrines of the royal ancestors,' said the emperor. 'I also must conduct the ceremonies to give thanks to gods of the earth and sky. I have so many

responsibilities. The people look to me as their ruler and protector. Yet I often feel so confused that I do not feel I can fulfill these obligations.

'I have made great sacrifices,' he went on, 'and have spoken with many men of knowledge and have studied the history of my family but I cannot seem to find a way to learn how to be the ruler that I wish to be.'

The old man stopped combing his beard and fixed his old yet surprisingly clear eyes on the emperor's. 'It takes someone who can manage his own life properly before he can expect to manage an entire country,' he said at last. 'I see before me a man full of doubt and worries, mostly put there by others in their own self-interest. And so I ask you, how, if the ruler's own life is in turmoil, can he expect to be able to rule a country properly?'

At this the emperor felt as though a great weight had been lifted off his shoulders. He felt that the scales had dropped from his eyes. Of course, he had been so concerned with his abilities as the ruler of the country he had given no thought to his own personal nature. Truly, if he were to be a wise and judicious ruler he must begin to know himself.

Thus began a lifelong journey into his own self-nature that not only enabled the emperor to rule his own country wise and well, but led him, at the end of his life, to be lifted to the heavens on the back of a golden dragon to sit by the side of the Jade Emperor himself.

SOLALA TOWLER

Why is the sea king of a hundred streams?

Because it lies below them.

Therefore it is the king of a hundred
streams.

If the sage would guide the people,
he must serve with humility,

If he would lead them he
must follow behind.

LAO TZU

Tale 18

The Craftsman and the Tao

Once there was a great craftsman who fashioned a mulberry leaf out of jade to give to the emperor. Hoping for a great reward, he worked on it for years, taking great care that it should be perfect.

Finally, after three long years, it was done. He placed it in a bowl along with other mulberry leaves. Its veins, its shape and its color were so realistic it could not be distinguished from a real one. The emperor was so impressed by the carver's work that he was immediately appointed to the royal court. Some time after that the carver lost favor with the fickle emperor and was dismissed.

When Lieh Tzu heard of this he said, 'If heaven and earth took so long to grow things that it took three years to grow a leaf there would not be many things with leaves.'

Therefore the follower of Tao puts her trust in the unfolding of the Way and not in cunning and skill.

LIEH TZU

This is why the sage embraces the one,

And serves as a model for everything
   under heaven.

In not showing off

She is seen by everyone.

In not being self-satisfied,

She is prominent.

In not being too aggressive

She accomplishes all her tasks.

In not boasting

She is admired by all.

Because she does not contend

No one contends with her.

The ancients said:

To yield is to become whole.

LAO TZU

117

The Magical Singer

The woman looked poor, dressed as she was in layers of rags to keep out the cold winds of winter. She was of indeterminate age, her hair bound up in another of her rags. But she looked the noodle vendor in the eye while she told him that she had no money to pay for his noodles yet she was very hungry.

'Be off with you,' cried the noodle man. He had seen enough beggars in his day and was in no mood for charity. He turned away from her and went back to waiting on his paying customers, ladling the thick noodle soup, filled with succulent pieces of fungus, vegetables and tasty chicken. But when he turned again the woman was still there. 'I thought I told you to be off,' he said, raising his soup ladle menacingly.

'Wait,' said the woman. 'I will trade you for the soup.'

The soup vendor eyed her suspiciously. 'And what, pray tell, have you to trade?'

'My songs,' she said and again looked him in the eye with that almost insolent look of hers.

A few of the other customers had been listening to this conversation and they now joined in. 'Yes,' they cried, 'let's hear her songs. We have heard no good music since the harvest festival last fall.'

The noodle vendor looked around at his smiling customers and decided, just this once, to give in. 'All right,' he said to the woman, 'but first the songs, then the food.'

'How can I sing when I am starving?' asked the woman. 'First feed me and then I will sing for you.'

The noodle vendor began to disagree but the other customers all shouted, 'Yes, feed her, feed her, and then she will sing for us.' So, he begrudgingly ladled out a small bowl of his soup for the starving woman and then stood behind his counter to watch her wolf it down as if she had not eaten for many days.

'More,' she said, handing back the bowl. The noodle vendor, of course, wanted to deny her but the other customers all shouted out, 'Give her more, then she will sing for us.' So he handed her another bowl.

It took a while, but finally after six servings of noodles, the woman set her bowl down on the counter and wiped her mouth with one of her rags and smiled at the noodle man and the other customers. She then sat down on a bench, alongside the others, and began to sing.

Her song was like no song anyone had ever heard. It seemed, at times, to be in another language entirely from the one spoken in that district, yet everyone could understand her. She didn't exactly sing words but rather some kind of phrases or sounds that spoke directly to the hearts of the listeners. Each one of them heard a slightly different song, as each one of them listened with their own ears and hearts. Even the scowling noodle vendor began to smile, and years of tension began to slide away from his face. More people began to fill the tiny room and soon they were standing around outside the building listening with rapt attention.

A man who had been about to commit suicide that night because of his loneliness was suddenly heartened and looked around at all the other villagers listening and said, 'Really, I am not so alone as I thought.' An old couple who had lost their children many years ago, suddenly saw them right in front of them and they laughed out loud. Another man who had been about to commit a murder that night found himself shaking with fear and asked himself, 'What was I thinking?' A woman who had been sick for many years and who had given up hope of ever recovering, suddenly felt new strength in her limbs and began to dance.

All who heard the magical voice of that poor, ragged woman, felt lighter, happier and calmer than they had felt for a long time. Soon everyone had closed their eyes, the better just to listen. The songs went on and on, winding their way down into the people's minds and hearts, down into the very root of their beings, down to where they were all small and often afraid. It lifted them then and brought them out to the glorious sunlight where they felt happy and safe.

Slowly the woman began to sing more and more softly. Then her voice became a sort of low hum. Several listeners opened their eyes then and saw, to their astonishment, that the woman was gone. But where was the sound coming from? They looked around themselves but could not see any sign of the woman. Still, the songs went on, soft and low and so beautiful it seemed as if it were the very gods themselves that must be singing.

After a while the noodle vendor himself looked up to the beams of the ceiling and it seemed as if he could make out the shadows of the traces of the songs up there, curling about the roof beams and raining down softly upon the people.

The songs continued for three days after that. Visitors came from far and wide to hear them. The noodle vendor sold many bowls of noodles and everyone who came for those three days left with a lighter and happier heart.

Much later, that same poor and ragged woman was still traveling. She was still very thin and she tried to bargain for a room in a small inn. It was very cold and she was afraid she would not last the night out in the open. But this time the innkeeper, a short and dried-up old man, would not listen to her pleas. When she tried to sing him a song to show him what she could do, he grabbed up a stick of firewood and began to beat her with it, shouting for her to get out of his inn.

She retreated then to the courtyard and, looking at him with a wild and awful stare, began to sing a song so sad and mournful that everyone in range of her voice felt tears running down their cheeks. They felt themselves suddenly become so weak that they had to sit down, for fear they would fall right there in the street. The innkeeper fell back into his inn, and wrapped an old quilt around his head to shut out the awful sounds.

The longer she sang the louder it seemed her song became and soon everyone in the quarter could hear her and was affected. She sang a song so sad and low that there was not a person there who did not feel suddenly hopeless and beaten down. Couples fell into each other's arms, weeping. Old people just crawled to their beds and prepared themselves for death. Even the children stopped their running and playing and began to cry, as if they had just lost their mother.

Long after the woman had left, trudging out into the cold, her song kept on going, swirling about the village like a malignant vapor cloud. Finally, after three days of this the village headman sent out a search party to find the woman and beg her to stop her song, lest everyone in the village commit suicide.

They found her out in the forest, half-frozen and near death. They carried her back to the very inn that she had been driven from and piled blankets upon her, heated bricks to warm her, and fed her strong nourishing soups until she had regained enough strength to take back her song.

She sat out in front of the inn then and began to sing. At first it was very difficult to hear her, she was so weak. But gradually, bit by bit, her voice became stronger and her song began to travel out into the village and everyone who heard it was suddenly cheered. Now her song seemed to revitalize everyone. It seemed to lift them out of their gloom and carry them out into the street.

From all parts of the village, people came dancing and waving their arms in the air. They gathered around the singing woman and began to sing along with her. She held her head up and, with tears running down her cheeks, she sang on and on into the night. A huge bonfire was built and people danced around it all night, listening to her song that filled them like good food; that reminded them of all the good things of life; that flowed through their veins like strong chi; that helped them to drop away their cares and woes like old clothing; that made them all feel years younger and somehow wiser.

When the mysterious singer had healed and was strong enough to resume her traveling she was sent off with great celebration and was never heard of in those parts again. But forever after, people from that village were famed for their ability to sing at weddings or funerals in such a way as to move their listeners to tears of joy or grief.

LIEH TZU

The softest thing in the universe

Overcomes the hardest thing in the
universe.

LAO TZU

Tale 20

The Great Awakening

People in general bustle about here and there. The sage seems stupid and without 'knowledge'. When people dream they do not know that they are dreaming. In their dream state they may even pretend to interpret dreams. Only when they truly awaken do they begin to know that they have been dreaming. By and by will come the Great Awakening, and then we shall find out that life itself is a great dream. All the while the fools think that they are awake, and that they have knowledge. They go on making distinctions, they differentiate between princes and grooms. How stupid!

CHUANG TZU

Tale *21*

A Celebration of Death

Upon hearing of the death of Chuang Tzu's wife, his good friend Hui Tzu went over to comfort him and found the sage sitting on the ground banging on an overturned pot and singing a song at the top of his lungs.

Horrified at such behavior, Hui Tzu reproved him, saying, 'This woman has lived with you, borne your children, grown old with you and now she has died. It is bad enough not to be weeping at this time but to be out here banging on a pot and singing is too much!'

Chuang Tzu replied, 'You are mistaken my friend, at first I could not help but feel sad and depressed at my beloved wife's death. But then I began to reflect. In the beginning, she had no life, and having no life she had no spirit, and having no spirit she had no body. But then she was given life, she was given a spirit and then she was given a body. Now things have changed again and she is dead. She has joined the great cycle of the seasons. Now she lies suspended between heaven and earth. Why then should I weep and moan over her. It would be as though I did not understand the process of life. Therefore I stopped and decided to celebrate.'

CHUANG TZU

Tale 22

Ai Tai To, the Ugly Man

Ai Tai To was an ugly man. That is true. As a matter of fact, he was more than ugly. He was monstrous. His head was huge, with thick black eyebrows that almost, but not quite, met in the middle. His brow likewise, was thick and stuck out from his forehead like a cliff. His nose was crooked, as were most of this teeth. His whole body seemed twisted and stumpy like an old tree trunk. His hands were huge, with thick hairy knuckles and blunt fingers like shovels. All in all he was a most ugly man. And yet ...

Ai Tai To had many friends it seemed. When I arrived at his village, all I had to do was speak his name and the faces of the villagers would light up. 'Ah, Ai Tai To, yes he lives here among us. And most fortunate are we. A greater friend and neighbor a man could never have.'

And most amazingly, when I would ask of some comely maiden, she would blush, cast down her eyes and say, 'Ah yes, Ai Tai To, such a man,' with such admiration and longing in her voice that I nearly fell off my horse with amazement.

Is this the Ugly Man that I have been searching for I wondered. How could this be? I had expected people to shudder at his name. I had certainly expected young maidens to shrink with revulsion at the very thought of him yet here they were, acting as if he were a prize catch!

I could see then that he was no ordinary man. Even if his exceedingly ugly features would be out of place in the elegant court surroundings I was used to, I knew that to have him there would make my life so much easier and richer. He had a way of listening to what I had to say with absolutely no judgment. He just soaked up what I was saying and then reflected it back to me like a mirror. I saw then that many of my deepest fears were really of little importance. His solutions, given in the fewest words possible, appeared so simple and so obvious that it seemed as though I had thought of them by myself. Later on, of course, I learned that he had spent years studying with various Taoist sages but back then I knew nothing about Taoist sages. Our teacher, Kongfuzi, had looked askance at Taoist sages as being wizards and charlatans and had warned us against having anything to do with them.

But after spending that morning with him I knew that I needed this man by my side. I invited him, I entreated him, I practically begged him to leave his little back-country village and travel with me to the court, where he would live in a great house and have servants, fine food and clothes. He, of course, refused. At the time I did not understand this. I thought him merely perverse or prideful or perhaps a bit frightened of the big city. But however much I offered to reward him, Ai Tai To made it very clear to me that he had no interest in living in the capital. He liked living in a small village where he knew everyone and everyone knew him. Perhaps he was a bit shy about his strange looks and how they would be received by the sophisticates in the capital, but I now know that he had a strong aversion to what he considered the artificial court life.

Later on he would explain to me that living in his simple fashion allowed him to feel closer to the Tao in all its manifest and unmanifest glory. His teachers, simple rough men and women he had met in the mountains where he had gone to gather wood to work into furniture, had shared much of their wisdom with him when he was young and impressionable and he had never forgotten it.

'Be like water,' they had told him. 'Water takes whatever shape it finds itself in. It does not judge, it does not complain, it does not try to change things. It is the source of patience. Given time it can wear away stone. Be like water.'

And further, 'Be like the young plants, pliant and supple. Plants, as they grow old, stiffen and become brittle and easily broken. Be like young plants.'

And still further, 'Be like a simple block of wood. Remember, when you search the forest for the right wood to build your furniture, how you look for certain qualities and characteristics. You look for the shape of the piece that you are going to build as if it is already in the wood itself. You too are a simple block of wood, with all your ineffable qualities and characteristics waiting there to be freed by your own spiritual practice. Be simple and natural like a block of wood.'

They told him these things and they showed him the simple yet profound writings of their teacher, Lao Tzu, the revealer of the Way, who had once been the royal archivist, in charge of the imperial library, who had sickened of a corrupt and cruel society and so had left for the far-off wilderness, never to be seen again. But before he went away he had left this small book of some of his teachings, to be shared with others - those who wanted to rule a country and those who wanted to rule themselves.

Ai Tai To was strong and robust, even by country standards. How he could maintain his health so well with the simple food of the country and his own often backbreaking labor I did not

140

understand. I, who had lived all of my life at court, could barely keep up with him when we went on a walk later that day. He stopped and showed me how to breathe 'from my heels'. He told me that if men only knew how to breathe properly, many of the diseases that laid waste to us all could easily be avoided.

I watched him as he moved among the trees, often reaching out and caressing a certain one. He would even murmur things to them, as if they were old friends. I saw too, how he moved like an animal there in the forest, not like a clumsy, noisy man, as I did. I saw that he was at home there, not as a man, but as a part of the forest itself.

When we returned to his hut I again entreated him to come with me, but again he refused. Finally, taking pity on me I believe, he said that he would come when winter arrived, since he would no longer be able to move through the forest as he liked anyway, with the snow and the cold. I rejoiced then and thanked him and would have given him gold right then but he refused it, saying he had not yet earned it. I should wait until he came to me and then see if he was worth anything at all.

I waited the rest of that year impatiently. I had arranged to obtain a copy of the book by Lao Tzu that Ai Tai To had shown me but had much trouble in understanding it. It seemed to be written in such simple yet abstruse fashion that I could make very little sense of it. I knew that there was something there for me but I could not find it. I know now that it was my own mind that got in my way. If I had been able to relax and just listen to the sage's words with my *shen* or spirit mind, I would have understood all that was there, just as Ai Tai To did. But this I did not learn until much later, after Ai Tai To had left me and it was too late.

Finally the day came when one of my guards announced that a very ugly and rude man had arrived, asking to see me. He had, of course, driven him away immediately. Beside myself, I pushed him aside and ran out of the palace searching for my friend. I found him in the marketplace, sitting with the craftspeople, comparing notes on woodworking and drinking wine. I led him back to my palace in front of my dumbfounded guards and into my inner chamber. There I prostrated myself at his feet, though he immediately drew me up.

I had been having much trouble with my rapacious neighbors and had great need of his counsel. He was able to help me then. He gave me good and useful advice, cutting through all the usual layers of false diplomacy and erroneous truths. I followed it and prospered.

Every day Ai Tai To would sit with me and give advice on the ruling of my kingdom, often quoting from Lao Tzu's work. 'Rule a kingdom as if cooking a small fish,' he once told me. 'If you interfere with it too much while cooking, it will fall apart and be inedible.'

In the evening he would sit with me and help to calm my mind and train my breathing. We would sit for hours, exploring deeply the wonders of the inner world of Tao. He became my confidant, my teacher, my counselor, and the best friend I ever had.

At first no one else in the palace trusted him. With his strange and even hideous looks they were sure that he was evil. But gradually they came under his spell, just as I had, just as the villagers in his own home had. Even my ladies-in-waiting, instead of shrinking back in revulsion as they had when he first arrived, began to ask about him wistfully and I found myself becoming a little jealous of him.

How he managed this transformation of people's regard of him I never truly understood. Of course to me he was useful and wise. He knew the ways of the human heart better than any man or woman I had ever known. Often it seemed that he was even able to use his ugliness in his own favor. Perhaps if he had been as handsome as he was wise, he would have become like most other men, crafty and selfish. Perhaps his suffering, as I am sure he must have suffered growing up with that face, had taught him something about the human condition that others did not know.

All I know is that, after the initial shock of seeing him for the first time, people relaxed and were able to open themselves to him, where they were unable to others, even me. Often I found him giving counsel or advice to various members of my court. He would accept no reward

from them, saying that he was being generously paid by me already and had no use for more gold. After all, there was no place to spend gold in the forest.

Eventually I began to rely upon him so greatly that one night I awoke with the idea that he, Ai Tai To, should be the ruler of my kingdom instead of me. I was overjoyed and humbled by this idea. I ran to him in the morning and joyously told him of my plan. I would hand over the reins of the state to him. I would remain, of course, in the court, but only as a sort of regent or second-in-command. I had expected him to share this vision with me and be as happy as I was. I was wrong.

His face clouded over as soon as I told him of my plans. For the first time I saw him as truly ugly. His features grew dark and bunched together. I was afraid he was becoming angry. I stopped speaking and watched him struggle with himself for a few moments. Then he began breathing deeply, his face unclenched and he looked again as my wise counselor and friend. 'I must think about this,' he told me, and turned away. 'Please, let me alone to think about this thing.'

I went away then and stayed away for the whole day. Of course, I thought, he is overwhelmed with my idea. After all, he is a simple rustic peasant. The thought of being a ruler is a very difficult thing for him to accept right away. I would wait until morning and approach him again.

But when I went to his chambers in the morning I found that he was gone. He had left in the night and no one had seem him go. I searched frantically for him throughout the whole town but he was not to be found. I even traveled again to his far-off village but no one there had seen him either.

Now, years later, I think I have begun to understand a little why Ai Tai To did not accept my offer and allow me to step down in his place. At first I thought it was that he was frightened of so great a responsibility but then I realized that he was not frightened of anything. I thought back to the first night that he spent here in the palace. How he had paced the floor of his splendid chambers like a wild animal and I thought then that he would bolt and return to his forest.

I had asked him what was wrong, were his quarters not comfortable enough? 'This is a trap,' he had answered, looking for a moment like a great bear. 'My friend, you have trapped me here and I do not know if I will be able to escape.'

I had stood, dumbfounded at this. 'Why would you want to escape from here?' I had asked, looking around at the sumptuous surroundings.

'Because I will lose myself in here with all these comforts. I will lose my sense of the Way and become lost in the world of dust and duty.'

I assured him then that he would be able to leave whenever he wanted. He seemed to calm down then and as the days passed, I thought that he had become more accustomed to his rich surroundings. But he had not.

He knew as soon as I offered to step down and give my throne to him that if he had accepted, he would be lost forever, just as I was. I knew that he had struggled with his sense of duty and obligation and even friendship for me. But at the end, he had chosen to be true to himself and for that I was, and am, glad.

Often I think of my ugly friend, as I grow ever older here in my palace. I think that I am a slightly better ruler than I was before, thanks to him. I often spend whole nights puzzling over passages of Lao Tzu's work and the older I get, the more I think I understand. It is at times when I am tired and feeling feeble-minded that I think I understand the most. I can often see my old friend's face then, with its ugly contours, lit up from within with the joy and wisdom of the Tao and I am grateful indeed for having know him but eternally sad that he had to go away.

CHUANG TZU

Surrender yourself
humbly;

Then you can be
trusted to care for
all things.

Love the world as
your own self;

Then you can truly
care for all things.

LAO TZU

His Cup Runneth Over

There was once a highly educated and somewhat arrogant student of the Way. Upon hearing that an old sage lived nearby he decided to visit so that he could show off his great depth of knowledge in hopes of gaining some new tidbit to add to his resume.

When he arrived at the sage's home he was surprised to find it but a humble hut. Inside, an old man with a long wispy beard and bright shining eyes sat over a tea kettle, humming to himself.

Presently he looked up and, upon seeing the student outside of his door, bade him enter his hut. He then sat the student down in the place of honor and asked the student to join him in some tea.

They sat, and while the student boasted about his education and recounted his many accomplishments, the old master began to fill his guest's teacup. As the student rambled on and on so too did the old master keep pouring tea into his cup until the hot tea overflowed across the table and poured onto the student's lap.

'What are you doing, you old dolt?' he shrieked, leaping from his chair. 'You are spilling tea everywhere. Can't you see that my cup is already full?'

The sage calmly stopped pouring tea and looked at him. 'Your mind, sir, is much like this teacup. I'm afraid it is already too full for me to be able to fit anything else into. Else it will surely run over and spill everywhere.'

TRADITIONAL

The sage keeps her wisdom to herself

While ordinary people flaunt their
knowledge.

CHUANG TZU

The Man Who Wanted to Forget

There was once a man by the name of Hua Zi who had lost his memory. It was said that if he was told a thing in the morning he would forget it by night. If you were to give him a present he would forget to take it with him. In the street he would stop suddenly, forgetting where he was going, forgetting even how to walk. When he finally arrived home he would stand in the middle of the room, forgetting where to sit. Each day he would forget what had happened the day before.

Naturally, his family was quite distraught. Admittedly, he did not seem too unhappy. As a matter of fact, he seemed quite at ease with his disease but the family was suffering, the family business was suffering, the family's name in the town was suffering and that was just too much.

So the family met and decided to call in various healers, diviners, and even sorcerers to see if they could effect a cure, but all to no avail. They called in a doctor of the medical arts, who, after feeling the old man's pulses and looking at his tongue, shook his head and said that there was nothing he could do for the patient. 'There is a wind in his *shen*,' he told them. 'His spirit is wandering far from here and I do not know how to call it back. His liver is out of accord with his spleen and his lungs and his kidneys are not in communication. I recommend giving up hope for a cure.' Then he charged them one gold piece for his examination and left the house.

Then one day the family was told about a certain philosopher, a man of high learning and erudition, who might be able to help them with their plight. So anxious for a cure was the family that when the philosopher, who, although he appeared on the young side for so high an office, demanded half their business as his fee, they agreed.

The philosopher was led into the chambers of the old man Hua Zi, who sat on the edge of his bed with a benign though vacant smile. The philosopher walked back and forth in front of Hua Zi for a time, pulling on his slight whiskers. He went over and peered into Hua Zi's ears, then his eyes, and then his nose. Satisfied he turned to the family, who had all gathered there.

'This disease cannot be cured by the usual methods,' he announced authoritatively. 'Yes, yes,' agreed the family. 'So we have been told.'

'Yes,' repeated the philosopher, 'this is a very serious case indeed. It cannot be cured with herbs, with incantations, with divination or any of the usual methods. It can only be cured by restoring his mind.'

Well, the family could not help but agree with this learned though very young philosopher. 'Yes,' announced the first-born, 'it is plain to see that it is his mind that is troubled. No wonder those other diviners, healers, and doctors where not able to cure him with all of their talk about his *feng shui* being out of balance, his five transformations being out of synch, his organs all being blown about by an internal wind. I could have told you as much, if you had asked me.' Here he gave the rest of the family the haughty glare of the first-born.

about the head and shoulders all the way. Then he turned on his poor old wife and drove her out of the room. His other family members begged him to be calm and cease his violent activities, whereupon he began beating them, all the while shouting in a very loud voice. Finally, when he had driven all the family members out of the house he took up his old hunting spear and went after the philosopher!

The philosopher ran speedily out of the house and into the street, shouting at the top of his lungs, 'Murder! Murder!' A few of the local constables heard his cries and came to his aid. Imagine their surprise when they found old, harmless, forgetful Hua Zi bearing down on the prostrate philosopher with a hunting spear!

They managed to disarm and arrest Hua Zi and dragged him down to the police station and charged him with attempted murder of the philosopher.

Upon being questioned as to his actions Hua Zi replied, 'When I lost my mind I was happy, carefree, and felt myself as boundless as the sky. When I slept I had no dreams, at least that I can remember, and I woke up each day into a new world. I had nothing on my mind and I felt like a free man. Now that I have my memory back, all my old problems and fears have come back to haunt me! I can now remember all the joy and sorrows, triumphs and troubles, and fortune and misfortune of my long life. There is no end to it.

'When I forgot myself I was happy, I was safe, I was serene. Now that I have my memory back I am miserable. I have woken up from my happy dream into a nightmare! Shall I never return to those happy days when my memory was lost?'

LIEH TZU

163

Where can I find a
man who has
forgotten words?

I would like to have
a word with him.

CHUANG TZU

Playing With The Fish

Chuang Tzu and his friend Hui Tzu were ambling about in the Garden of Perpetual Harmony one fine day. Their conversation ranged from how lovely the weather had been lately to the art of compounding herbal preparations for longevity. Hui Tzu was of the opinion that one could not only live a long and healthy life by ingesting these formulas, many of which contained poisonous minerals, but could attain immortality. Chuang Tzu, on the other hand, was of the opinion that what he called 'all this grasping after immortality' was a waste of time and utter foolishness.

'We are already immortal,' he would say to his friend. 'As we are all part of the great unending and constantly transforming Tao, our immortality is assured. There is no need to ingest noxious brews or stretch ourselves into strange and painful contortions in order to attain immortality. Just live your life in accordance with the Tao and your immortality will manifest of itself.'

But Hui Tzu was not convinced. 'If that were true,' he argued, 'then every blockhead that lives is really an immortal.'

'Just so,' answered Chuang Tzu.

At one point, when they were crossing the Hao river, which was spanned by an ancient and lovely moon bridge, Chuang Tzu said to his

friend, 'These fish we see below us come out and swim about so leisurely. This is the joy of fishes.'

Hui Tzu turned to him and said, 'How do you know what fish enjoy, you're not a fish!'

'You are not me,' answered Chuang Tzu, 'so how do you know what I know about the joy of fish?'

'Well,' said his friend somewhat indignantly, 'I am not you and so do not know what you know. But, as you are certainly not a fish, there is no possible way that you can know what fish enjoy.'

'Ah, then,' said Chuang Tzu, who was letting his fingers play slowly in the water as little fishes came up to nibble them. 'Let us go back to the beginning of our conversation. When you asked me "How can you know what fish enjoy?" you knew that I knew. The reason I know this is by walking over the river!'

As was the usual case in these kinds of conversations, Hui Tzu glared at his friend, who was languidly moving his fingers in the water and chuckling to himself.

CHUANG TZU

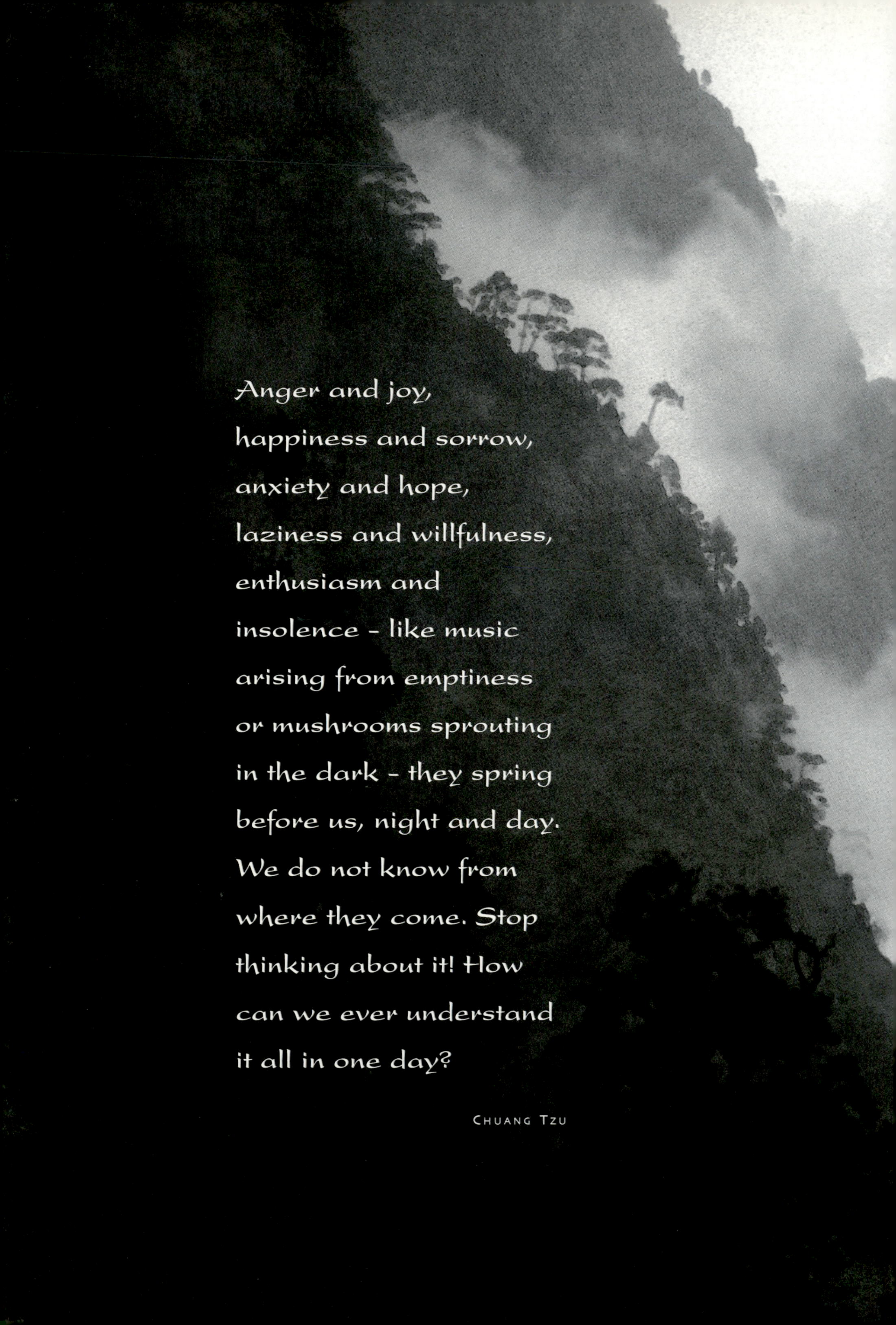

Anger and joy,
happiness and sorrow,
anxiety and hope,
laziness and willfulness,
enthusiasm and
insolence – like music
arising from emptiness
or mushrooms sprouting
in the dark – they spring
before us, night and day.
We do not know from
where they come. Stop
thinking about it! How
can we ever understand
it all in one day?

CHUANG TZU

feet trod. He did not notice what thought came into his head and what his words contained.

It was then that he began to drift with the wind like a leaf blown from a tree. And he was not able to distinguish whether he was riding the wind or if the wind was riding him.

If we could only become like Lieh Tzu the principles of all things would be revealed to us!

LIEH TZU

The sage knows without learning,

sees without looking, achieves
  without striving,

and understands without trying.

Sages act only when necessary,

move only when there is no choice.

They are like rays of light.

HUAINANZI

Tale 27

A Beautiful Illusion

The master had preached for many years that life was but an illusion.
Then, when his son died, he wept. His students came to him and said,
'Master, how can you weep so when you have told us so many times
that all things in this life are an illusion?'

'Yes,' said the master, wiping away his tears while they continued to
course down his ancient cheeks, 'but he was such a beautiful illusion!'

CHUANG TZU

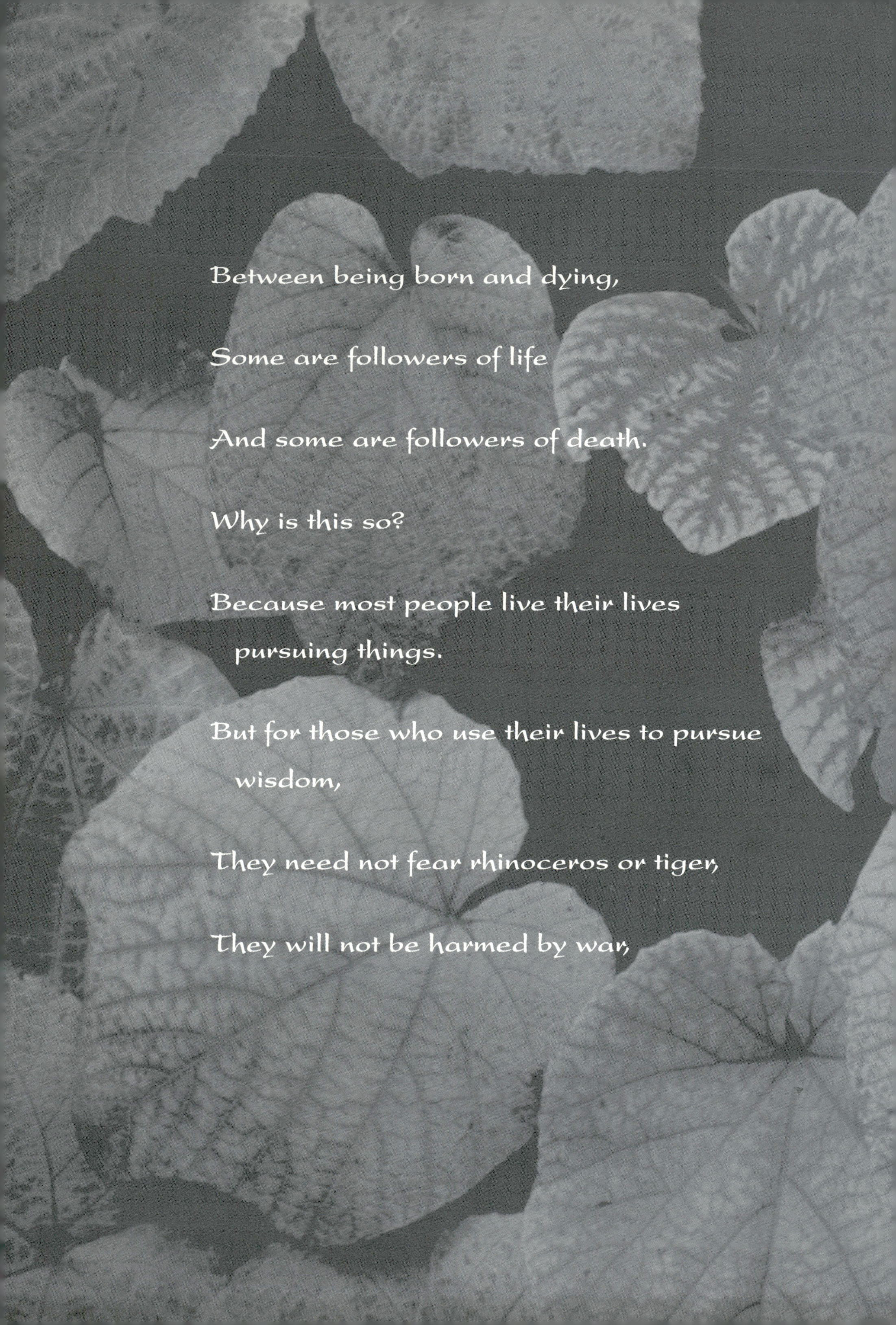

Between being born and dying,

Some are followers of life

And some are followers of death.

Why is this so?

Because most people live their lives
    pursuing things.

But for those who use their lives to pursue
    wisdom,

They need not fear rhinoceros or tiger,

They will not be harmed by war,

This is because the rhinoceros has no place

To thrust his horn.

The tiger has no place

To sink his claws.

A weapon has no place to pierce.

Why is this so?

Because such people have no place for death
  to enter.

LAO TZU

Tale *28*

True Beauty

Yang Chu was traveling, and at the end of a long day, he put up at an inn that sat by the raging course of a river. He was dog-tired yet when he entered the inn he could not help but notice that the innkeeper, an old and very fat man, had two wives - one very young and beautiful, the other somewhat older and very ugly.

After he had been served a simple yet filling meal he congratulated the innkeeper on the beauty of his young wife. 'Ah,' replied the innkeeper, 'that one is so proud of her beauty that it is hard for me to see her as beautiful. On the other hand, my old wife is very ugly indeed but she is so accepting and untroubled by it that I cannot see her ugliness and regard her as beautiful.'

When Yang Chu returned home he told his students about this and admonished them. 'To be truly worthy you must give up all ideas and concepts of worthiness. Do not dwell on your accomplishments and you will be held in the highest esteem by those around you.'

CHUANG TZU

Going with the Flow

Once Confucius was looking down into a gorge where a great waterfall crashed down to a huge roiling chasm so violent that no fish, tortoises or even alligators could survive there. Suddenly he noticed an old man appear to tumble over the falls into the maelstrom. Horrified, Confucius, along with several of his disciples, ran downstream in hope of saving the poor unfortunate, only to find him strolling merrily along the bank, singing to himself.

Cautiously, Confucius approached the old man and said to him, 'I thought at first that you were some sort of spirit, but now I can see that you are a man of flesh and blood. Tell me, how in the world did you manage to survive that plunge into the river?'

'Oh that,' answered the man. 'That is simple. I merely entered the water at the center of its whirl. I let myself flow along with it, not trying to impose my will upon it, then I left when it whirled the opposite way. It is all completely natural to me.'

'What do you mean by this?' asked Confucius. 'How can this be natural to you?'

'Well,' answered the man, already beginning to wander off again, 'I grew up on dry land and so am at home upon it. At the same time, I also grew up by the river and so am at home in the water. I don't really know how I do these things, I just do them. Therefore my success is assured.'

CHUANG TZU

187

Who can be still while the muddy water
settles?

Who can remain still until the time
comes for action?

LAO TZU

Tale 30

Possessing the Tao

There was once a diligent and serious student of the Way, who one day asked his master, 'Can you possess the Tao?'

'You can't possess even your own body,' answered his master. 'How could you possess the Tao?'

'If I don't possess my own body,' asked the student, 'then who does?'

'It has been lent to you by heaven and earth. Life itself is not your possession,' said his master. 'You don't possess your own nature or your own destiny. They have been lent to you by heaven and earth. Your children and their children are not your possession. They are as molted insect skins, lent to you by heaven and earth. So when you walk you don't notice where you are going, when you stop you don't know where you are. When you eat you don't know what it is that you are eating. The *chi* of heaven and earth is so much stronger than yours but even it can't posses the Tao.'

CHUANG TZU

When the superior person hears of the Tao

He diligently studies it.

When the inferior person hears of the Tao

Sometimes she remembers it, sometimes not.

When foolish students hear of the Tao

They laugh at it.

If they did not laugh at it,

It would not be the Tao.

LAO TZU

A Point of View

There was once a poor woodcutter who made his living cutting firewood in the forest to sell in the town. One morning he woke up, had his tea and rice gruel and went to take up his ax in order to go into the forest. But he could not find it anywhere. He searched high and low, inside and out but could not find it.

Oh no, he thought to himself, someone has stolen it! Just then he noticed the man who lived next door walking by. As he looked at him the woodcutter seemed to notice, for the first time, how shifty he looked. His eyes seemed to dart back and forth and he walked with his head down and his shoulders scrunched together and moved in a crab-like way down the lane.

It's funny, the woodcutter thought, that I have never before noticed how guilty and downright criminal my neighbor looks. As the neighbor scuttled off, the woodcutter decided to follow him. On and on they went until, as the sky passed slowly overhead, the woodcutter suddenly lost sight of the thieving neighbor.

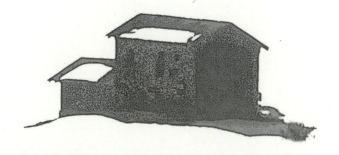

Drat, he thought, I've lost him! He's probably gone to visit his hideout, where he keeps all his stolen goods. The woodcutter waited awhile, in case the thief showed up again but finally he decided to go on home and confront the thief when he showed up again.

As he walked home, the woodcutter reflected on his neighbor. It was funny that he had never noticed before now, what a bad egg his neighbor was. To think that for all this time he had lived next door to a thief!

When the woodcutter arrived home he went to hang up his coat when his foot collided with something heavy and sharp on the floor behind the rice basket. Looking down, he found, to his amazement, that it was the missing ax. He must have left it there the night before when he had been preparing dinner.

Just then the neighbor was seen returning home. As the woodcutter stood there, ax in hand, he noticed that a friendly and open face now replaced the guilty, shiftless look he had seen earlier. His head and shoulders were a bit lopsided, it was true, but that was probably due to the heavy work he did carrying bales of rice all day down at the marketplace.

The neighbor waved to the woodcutter as he went by but the woodcutter turned away, weighed down with shame for his own thoughts about this innocent man.

LIEH TZU

Best be still, best be empty.

In stillness and emptiness we find
    where to abide;

Talking and giving, we lose the place.

LIEH TZU

Tale 32

Progress on the Path

Yen Hui came to his master and said, 'I am making progress in my cultivation.'

'In what way?' asked his master.

'I have forgotten the rituals and the music.'

'That is good,' said his master, 'but it is not enough. Keep working.'

A few days later Yen Hui came back and said, 'I am doing even better.'

'And how is that?' asked his master.

'I have forgotten about humaneness and righteousness.'

'Ah,' said his master. 'Very good, but still not good enough. Back to work.'

Then Yen Hui came before his master once again. 'This time I think I have it,' he said.

His master sighed. 'What is it this time?' he asked.

'I have learned how to sit and forget.'

At this the master pricked up his ears. 'What do you mean by sitting and forgetting?' he asked.

'Well,' said Yen Hui. 'I have learned to let go of my body, quiet my mind, and become as one with the infinite. This is what I call sitting and forgetting.'

'Aha,' said the master, bowing to Yen Hui. 'I see you have indeed attained the Way. Now it is my duty to follow after you.'

CHUANG TZU

Thirty spokes share one hub;

It is the empty space within that makes
  it useful.

Clay is shaped into a vessel;

It is the empty space that makes it
  useful.

Cut out doors and windows

And it is the empty spaces created that
  makes them useful.

Profit comes for what is there;

Usefulness by what is not there.

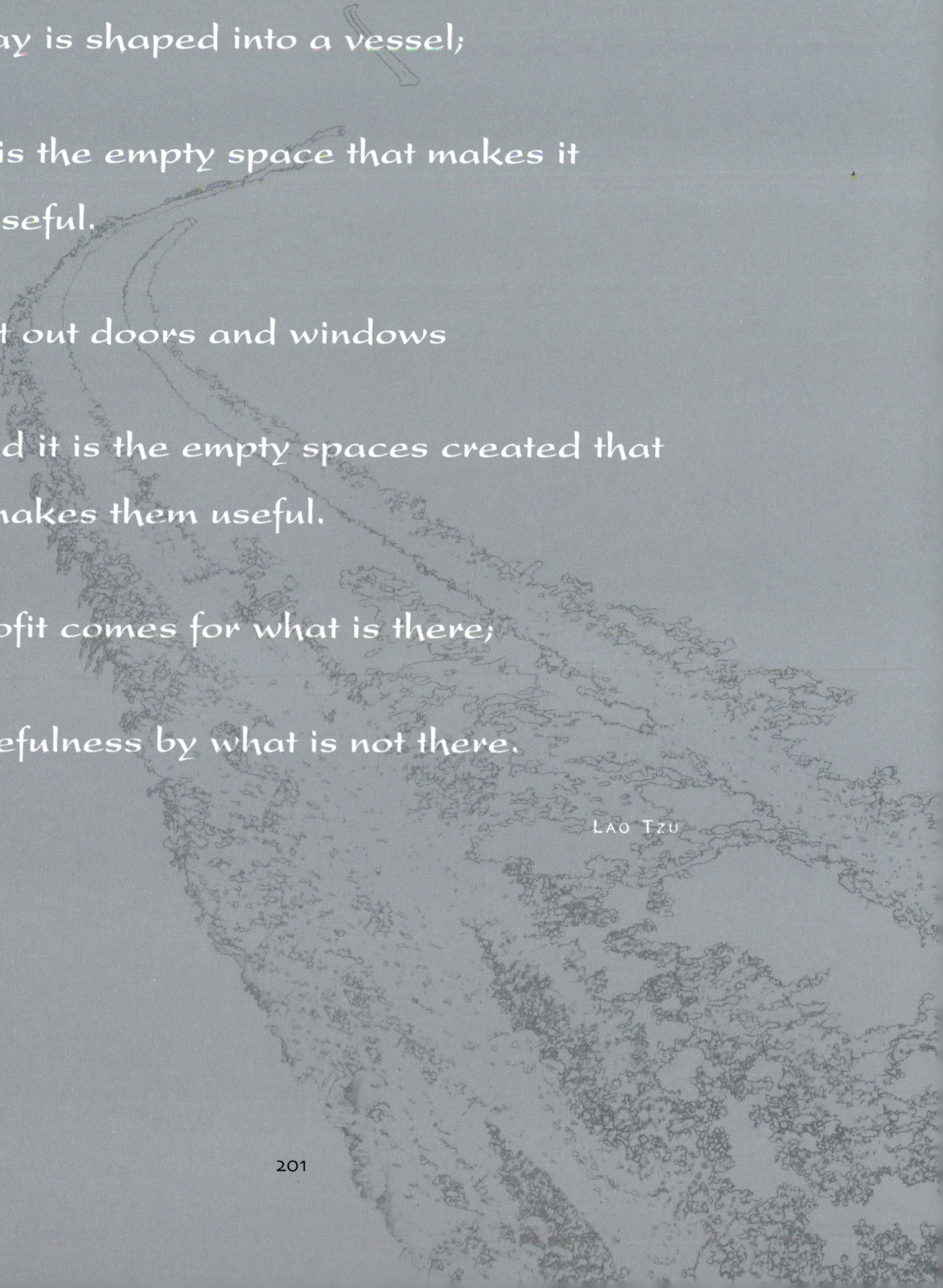

The emptiness between

heaven and earth is

like a bellows.

It is empty but does not

lose its form.

It can be moved but it

stretches even further.

Words do not count,

Maintain the center.

LAO TZU

Love Blooms, Then Fades

In ancient China there lived a beautiful woman named Mi Tzu-hsia, who was the favorite of the Lord of Wei. At that time, according to the law, anyone found riding in the lord's carriage without his permission was punished by having their foot cut off. Once, when Mi Tzu-hsia's mother became ill, she was so upset that she immediately set out in the lord's carriage to see her, without consulting him. But when the lord found out he only praised her for her filial devotion. 'Imagine,' he said, 'risking such a severe punishment for her mother!'

One day while she and her lord were walking in the garden, Mi Tzu-hsia picked a ripe peach and, finding it delicious, she gave it to her lord to finish. Again he praised her, saying how much she must love him to forget her own pleasure to share it with him.

But, years later, as Mi Tzu-hsia's beauty began to fade, she fell out of favor with her lord. Then one day, when she had done something to offend him he rebuked her saying, 'I remember how she once took my carriage without my permission. And another time she gave me a peach that she had already bitten into!'

Thus did the Lord of Wei's love for Mi Tzu-hsia fade like a flower in the fall.

LIEH TZU

Returning is the direction of the Tao.

Yielding is the way of the Tao.

All things under heaven are born of
being; being is born of non-being.

LAO TZU

Tale 34

True Forgetfulness

Clubfoot-Hunchback-No-Lips came to see Duke Ling. After speaking together, Duke Ling became so delighted with him that when he looked at normal people, it seemed to him that their backs looked stiff and straight, their legs looked thin and spindly and their lips looked too full.

Jug-Neck-Goiter came to see the Duke of Chi. He so impressed the duke that when he saw normal people he thought their necks looked thin and scraggy.

When one's personal integrity shines forth, one's outward appearance will be forgotten. Not forgetting what should be forgotten and forgetting what should not be forgotten - that is called true forgetfulness!

CHUANG TZU

The highest good is like water.

Water gives life to the ten thousand
things and does not strive.

It flows in places men reject and so is
like the Tao.

LAO TZU

Tale 35

The Curse of Fame

Lieh Tzu was on his way to Chi but decided to turn back when he had gone halfway. He met his master along the way who asked him why he had turned back.

'I was alarmed by something,' he replied. Lieh explained that at every inn he was served first.

'Why was that such a problem?' asked his master.

'When a man's inner integrity is not firm,' said Lieh Tzu, 'something oozes out of his body and becomes like an aura about him and presses on the hearts of others. It makes other men honor him more than his elders and betters and gets him into difficulties.'

He then went on to describe that the motive of the innkeeper was to sell his wares and to make his profit. 'If such a man as this values me so highly,' he said, 'think of how much worse it will be when the great lord finds out about me. He will appoint me to some office and insist that I fill it efficiently. This is what has alarmed me.'

'An excellent way to look at it,' said the master. 'But there is no way out of it. Even if you stay, other men will lay responsibilities upon you.'

Another time Lieh Tzu's master came to see him and found the

doorway crowded with the shoes of visitors. When he turned to leave, Lieh Tzu saw him and ran after him and asked him if he had come to give him his blessing.

'Enough,' thundered the master. 'I told you confidentially that others would lay responsibilities on you, and it turns out so they have.'

He then said a very curious thing. 'It is not that you are capable of allowing them to do it to you but that you are incapable of preventing them. What use is it to you to have this effect on people, which is so incompatible with your own peace? If you insist of having an effect, it will unbalance your true nature and to no purpose.'

LIEH TZU

Give up sagehood, renounce wisdom

And the people will benefit a hundredfold.

LAO TZU

Tale 36

The Natural Order of Things

When the master died, Chin Shih came to the funeral, looked around and shouted three times. One of the other disciples said, 'I thought you were a friend of the master.'

'Yes, of course I am,' replied Chin Shih.

'Well, do you think it proper to behave this way?' asked the disciple.

'Yes,' said Chin Shih. 'When I first walked into the room I thought that the master's spirit was still here. Now I see that it is not. I came

prepared to mourn but, upon seeing everyone here wailing at the top of their lungs, I realized that this was all wrong. This is ignoring the natural course of things.

'The master came because it was his time. When it was time for him to leave, he left. If we ourselves are also content to follow the natural flow there would be no room for grief. This is truly freedom from bondage. When the wood burns the wood itself is consumed, to where it goes we cannot say.'

CHUANG TZU

Those who know that
   they have enough
   are wealthy.

Those who go hold their
   place have great power.

Those who do not lose
   their place will endure.

To die but not to perish is
   to be eternally present.

LAO TZU

Tale *37*

Tasting for Tea

There is a well-known story about Lu Yu, a famous tea master who was an expert on what kind of water was best for brewing tea. He actually wrote a book on twenty sources for the water to be used for brewing tea. The best, he said, was from midstream on the Yangtze at Nanling

Once, on a river trip with a local dignitary, he was given water from that spot to taste. Upon tasting it Lu Yu said that the water was not from midstream but from closer to the shore.

'But that cannot be,' said his host. 'I am sure it was taken from midstream. I ordered it so myself.'

'Perhaps,' conceded the master, 'but there is some other water mixed into it, perhaps from another part of the river.'

Later it was discovered that some of the water from the container had been lost when the boat had rocked and the servant had replaced it with water taken from nearer the shore.

Thus was the wisdom of the old masters both deep and all-encompassing. If they could taste the difference between one part of the river and another, how profound was their understanding of the Tao?

SOLALA TOWLER

Use the light to return to the Light.

Then you can die yet be ever living.

LAO TZU

Many words are not as good

as a few.

Maintain the center.

LAO TZU

The Way of Wu Wei

Once upon a time, in the Land of the Middle Kingdom, there lived a great emperor. This mighty lord lived in a magnificent castle, surrounded by many guards, ladies-in-waiting, cooks, artists, philosophers and doctors. He awoke each day to the soft caresses of one of his many wives, ate his breakfast in a wonderful garden

surrounded by the morning song of his many birds, and passed his days in the company of his many admirers and flatterers. But he was not happy.

He felt that he was missing out on some essential thing of life. Just what this essential thing was he did not know, but he knew that he did not have it, and this distressed him endlessly. He filled his court with various magicians and philosophers, all of whom tried to tell him that if

he would only listen to them and them alone he would find this essential and missing ingredient of his life. But he knew that each was only trying to better his own individual situation, and so did not heed their shining and flattering words.

Instead, he winnowed them out, one by one, until there were only two groups left, the Confucians and the Daoists. But he could not decide which one of them had the secret and essential thing that he was lacking. The Confucians were a haughty yet wise lot. They did not flatter him in silken phrases like the other philosophers had. They told him where his character was lacking and how he only had to reinstate the old rituals and he would be fine. They told him of the mighty days of old, when the emperor was truly the son of heaven and could rule in heaven's name. All he had to do was return to those days and revive the ancient ways of the old rites and rituals and his kingdom would prosper - he would be happy and fulfilled, both as a ruler and a man.

The Daoists, on the other hand, seemed an unorganized and motley crew. They never seemed to agree on anything, even among themselves and spent their days performing strange movements like animals, in the garden; their nights drinking wine, reciting poetry and trying to seduce his ladies-in-waiting. But they were said to have great powers over the

elements and the secret of eternal life. Of course, when he questioned them about this they only shrugged and said, 'We have but one precious secret and one only, my Lord.'

'Well then,' he would say, 'what is this precious thing?'

'Ah,' they would counter, 'we cannot describe this secret in words, great and powerful Lord, we can only show it to you.'

'Agreed,' said the emperor, and announced a contest between the Confucians and the Daoists. Whichever could show him the true secret of their power, he said, would become the supreme teachers of the land.

On the appointed day, the Confucians and the Daoists were led to a great chamber deep in the heart of the castle. A great curtain was drawn down the center of the room, dividing the Daoists from the Confucians. Both groups were told that they were to create a painting, a great work of art, on the wall on either side. This would be the final test of their power and knowledge. Whoever impressed the emperor the most would be awarded the prize.

The Confucians smiled and quickly ordered all the colors that were available in the royal storerooms. They immediately went to work designing and painting a magnificent mural. The Daoists, on the other hand, ordered a great deal of wine and a few dozen soft cloths, the softest that were available. Then they went to work on opening the wine.

Day after day the Confucians labored on their huge and wondrous mural. Day after day the Daoists ordered more wine and simply rubbed the wall with their soft cloths, over and over, while singing old drinking songs at the top of their lungs.

Finally came the day when the emperor would view each work of art and make his decision. First he visited the Confucians' side of the room, certain that he would be in for a visual treat. He had watched how assiduously the Confucians had applied their layers of colors on the wall and how they stopped often to study the ancient texts and perform slow and stately rituals before taking up their brushes again.

He was not disappointed. The Confucians had created a marvel of color and form. He saw his whole city laid out before him, with his own castle in the very center of the city, the golden light of the setting sun glinting off its shapely and graceful roofs. At the edge of the painting he saw his own magnificent form astride his favorite war horse, leading his victorious troops into battle against an already vanquished enemy. A great river ran across the bottom of the painting with cunning little waves painted all over it and the curly shadows of birds suspended above it. It was truly a wondrous and amazing sight and the emperor was at a loss as to how the Daoists could top it.

Imagine his surprise then when he crossed over to the other side of the room to view the Daoists' work only to find a completely blank wall and a lot of slightly tipsy Daoists doing their strange cloud-like movements. True, the wall was very shiny and smooth after numerous applications with the soft cloths but there was nothing there, no paintings of his magnificence, no golden palace, no wondrous river. 'What is this,' he thundered, 'you did not even try to paint a picture. Is this the way you curry my favor?'

'Oh but we have done our best!' cried the Daoists indignantly, and a little rudely.

'But there is nothing there,' said the emperor. 'Is this truly how you view me? Is this your precious secret?'

'Wait one moment please,' said the oldest and tipsiest of the Daoists, his long beard still damp with wine. 'Please draw aside the curtain between our walls and you will then truly see our work.'

So shaking his head in wonder, the emperor had the curtain drawn, revealing the dazzling painting of the Confucians. The emperor stood before it once again, marveling at its wonder (and how they seemed to get his noble brow just so). Then, his mind already made up as to who was the winner this day, he turned once again to the Daoists' blank wall, only to find there, not a blank wall after all but the reflection of the painting on the opposite wall. Only this time, instead of a flat and static picture, he saw reflected in the unbelievably smooth and shiny wall, a *moving* picture.

Somehow, because of the play of light on the shiny surface there, it seemed as though the painting had come alive. There was the palace and the town again, only he thought he could detect movement behind its windows. The river itself moved, the waves lapping against each other and the birds pirouetting overhead. And lastly, he could see himself there, astride his great stallion, whose very nostrils seemed to quiver in the air while his own beard fluttered in the breeze and his lips seemed to move with his own shouted orders to his troops.

He was amazed. He was astounded. He turned to the tipsy Daoists and asked them with humility and wonder in his voice just how they had managed this miracle. The Daoists seemed to hang their heads just a little and answered simply. 'It is actually in *not doing* that we have achieved this wondrous thing, Sire. All we did was create the space for the painting to happen and let it paint itself.'

'Is this then your precious secret?' asked the great lord.

'Yes,' answered the Daoists, 'it is indeed. We call it *wu wei* or 'not doing', and it is in creative and natural 'not doing' that we are able to achieve the highest level possible.' Then they turned and bowed in unison to the dumbfounded Confucians. 'We congratulate you noble sirs in your great work of art. We watched you every day work so diligently while we drank wine and rubbed a blank wall. What you have created is truly marvelous. But with your industry you have only created a flat and lifeless thing, while we, in our formlessness, have created a living world.'

It was said that afterwards, for the length of his reign, the emperor gave the Daoists in his kingdom his royal ear and they taught him many things until the day came for him to ascend to the heavens on the back of a dragon to take his place in the realm of the immortals.

SOLALA TOWLER

Other people have more than enough

But I alone seem to have lost everything.

I am foolish!

Other people are clear

While I alone am confused.

Other people are clever

While I am stupid.

I feel lost at sea,

Tossed about on the winds of a storm.

Everyone else has things to do,

While I am dull and stupid.

I am different from the others.

I am nourished by the Great Mother.

LAO TZU

Tale *39*

Direct Experience

The student came up to the master. 'This thing you call Tao,' he said, throwing wide his arms. 'Where does it exist?' The master stood for a moment then pointed to a steaming pile of ox manure at his feet. 'It is there,' he said.

The student asked the master, 'Master, what is the true meaning of Tao?' The master raised his staff and the student gave a shout. The master then struck his student with the staff. Another student also asked the master, 'Master, what is the real meaning of Tao?' The master again raised his staff. The student shouted and then the master also shouted. Then, as the student did not reply, he whacked him with the staff.

A student asked the master, 'I do not ask you anything about pointing, what is the moon?' The master asked back, 'Who is not asking about pointing?' Another student asked, 'I do not ask you about the moon, what is pointing?' The master answered, 'The moon.' The student then said, 'I asked about pointing, why did you speak of the moon?' The master answered, 'Because you asked about pointing.'

A student once asked Hsiang Yen, 'What is Tao?' Hsiang Yen replied, 'A dragon hums inside a withered log.'

The student came to the master and said, 'Please help me to quiet my mind.' The master answered, 'Bring me your mind and I promise I will help you.' The student stood there for a moment and then said, 'But Master, I cannot seem to find it.' 'Ah,' replied the master, 'then I already quieted it.'

TRADITIONAL

The Tao is hidden by partial understanding.

The true meaning of words is hidden by
flowery rhetoric.

CHUANG TZU

A Wandering Taoist

The cold wind blowing off the western desert ruffled the beard of the old man riding slowly atop the water buffalo. It whipped around his traveling cloak and made him shiver deep within his robes. He tried wrapping the cloak a little tighter around his shoulders but it did him little good. It was a bad time of the year for traveling, but that could not be helped. The stolid beast plodded on slowly toward the frontier. A horse would have been faster, but this beast was steadier, more sure-footed in the mountains and ate very little. He supposed it was a bit of reverse vanity that prompted him to travel on so humble a mount, the last vestige of the once proud royal archivist.

This man, called Lao Tan, was leaving his post and his life in court behind him and heading toward the western frontier. Life in the capital had been going from bad to worse. In fact, as far as he was concerned, society as a whole was falling apart. The court intrigue nauseated him, the constant political maneuvering gave him a headache, and it seemed as though cynicism was trickling down even into the lower classes. The tradesmen and shopkeepers were far more interested in making money than in being of good service. Even the farmers, the bedrock of civilization, were showing signs of dissatisfaction and doubt about their own lives.

Everywhere he looked Lao Tan saw signs that society was askew. It seemed to him that the Way had truly been lost and that things were only going to get worse. Even his students had become cynical, more interested in acquiring mystical powers than simply learning how to live in accord with the eternal Way. As if there were anything more powerful than that.

Armies were massing all along the borders of the various fiefs, ready to go at each other's throats at a moment's notice. And no longer were there chivalrous knights errant as in days past, seeking to redress the wrongs suffered by the weak at the hands of the rapacious strong. The ancient rules of combat in which battles were fought by favorites, thus avoiding needless bloodshed, were being ignored. Now, armies went at each other in wholesale slaughter, while the poor peasants whose lands they ravaged in battle suffered the loss of their crops, their sons and even their daughters to the bloodthirsty soldiers.

All in all, it had seemed like a good time to leave the festering swamp that society had become and head into the wilderness to pass his days in contemplation of the Way. So he had said goodbye to his students and his position, and since his wife had left this world of dust years before, he mounted his sturdy buffalo, and along with one of his most trusted and promising students carrying his *qin*, slowly plodded toward the setting sun.

As he traveled further and further from the capital it seemed to Lao Tan that he was able to breathe easier and his mind, so long cluttered with the endless minutiae of imperial service, became clear. He had wielded great power and greater responsibility as Keeper of the Archives in the capital. The people of the Middle Kingdom had long venerated the sacred power of the written word and, as Lao Tan was in charge of the imperial library, his was a most glorious post. Or so it had seemed in the beginning.

But after years of watching the supposedly learned men of the kingdom calcify their minds with mindless repetition of the writings of those who had come before them, never venturing an original idea or thought, lest it get them in trouble with the intelligensia of the court, he had begun to sicken of the life at the imperial court. He longed to breathe the air of mountains, to feel himself imbued with the *de* or sublime energy of those lofty places. He longed to sit with men and women who were not afraid to speak their minds, not afraid to dig deep into themselves for truth, knowledge, and experience of the ineffable and absolute Way.

And so he had mounted his buffalo, with its greenish tinge, and saying a few last goodbyes to his students and few friends, had set out on this slow and ponderous way, feeling freer than he had for many years.

Of course, as he traveled he came to towns where he was known, and men there - ostentatious, wealthy, and shallow men - tripped each other up to be able to feast and fete him, believing that he still had power and connections in the capital. Often he let them have their fantasies, especially when his student was half-starved and freezing from their journey, and let his officious hosts wine and dine them.

He was careful to promise them nothing but he could see the greed in their eyes as they sat with him, asking for his teaching while ignoring his very words of truth. 'Empty your minds and fill your bellies,' he had told them. And they, misunderstanding his words said, 'Yes, yes, take more of our humble and miserable food. Fill your belly with our unworthy dishes,' while serving him on gold platters.

But now, at last, he was past all the towns and cities of the kingdom, out on the edge of the wilderness, where he planned to live out his last days in peace, stillness, and quiet communion with the Tao. He had one last barrier to pass, one last test of his resolve.

At the end of the day he reached the outermost gate of the kingdom. He slowly and stiffly dismounted and turned to the gatekeeper who had come out of his tiny hut to greet him. Yinhi was a longtime friend and student and was about as old as Lao Tan himself.

'Master Lao,' he said, coming forward, his wrinkled face breaking into a broad smile. 'It's so good of you to visit. Are you on a vacation from the capital?'

'No,' answered Lao Tan, 'I'm afraid I'm done with all that. I am on my way out there.' He pointed to the vast desert on the other side of the pass.

Yinhi frowned. 'But that way is very hard, and may even mean your death.'

 'No matter,' said Lao Tan. 'It is time for me to leave my old life behind
and see what the Tao has in store for me.'

Later, after a simple but delicious meal, Lao Tan and his friend sat by
the fire and listened to the night sounds around them.

'Master Lao,' began Yinhi, 'if you are really going, never to return, I beg
you to please write something for your students so they may have
some of your wisdom to refer to in the troubled times ahead.'

'I am afraid that if they did not hear me when I was speaking to them, they surely will not listen to mere words on paper,' answered Lao Tan.

Lao Tan's student sat in the shadows and did not say anything. He had already exhausted all his words in begging his master for written instructions. That is why he had elected to accompany him out to the wilderness, away from his easy life in the court and out to who knows where, as long as he could stay by his teacher's side.

'But,' entreated Yinhi, 'if things are really getting as bad as you say, then we will surely be in need of whatever wisdom you can leave us.'

'I dislike writing things down,' answered Lao Tan, getting up and stretching. 'I feel there is really no way to convey the immensity of the Way in simple words, no matter how clever or polished. Now I must go to bed, old friend. I will be leaving at first light.'

Before going to bed, Lao Tan sat awhile, thinking over what Yinhi had said. He did feel a little guilty about leaving his students and friends back at the capital. Perhaps writing a few lines would not be such a bad thing after all. It might even help him formulate his thoughts a little better in his own mind. He got out his writing implements and began mixing his ink. Then, with his brush poised over a long strip of bamboo, he stopped.

How could he possibly put into words the immensity and depth of the Way? How could he, in a few lines, bring forth all that he had experienced and learned in a lifetime of seeking the great and sublime Tao? For a moment the thought overwhelmed him. But even though he was quitting this sad and misguided world, he felt responsible to the people who were struggling under the weight of fear and ignorance. If it was possible to leave behind a small token of his concern for them, he felt he had a duty to do what he could.

And so, after taking one deep breath 'from the bottom of his heels' he put his brush to the bamboo and began to write.

'The Tao that can be described is not the eternal Tao.
The name that can be spoken is not the eternal name.'

SOLALA TOWLER

When the great Tao is
    abandoned,

Benevolence and morality
    arise.

When wisdom and
    intelligence arise

There comes a great
    falseness.

When the family is not
    united,

Filial piety and kindness
    arise.

When the country is full of
    confusion and disorder,

Then loyal court ministers
    appear.

LAO TZU

249

Solala Towler has been teaching Taoist philosophy and practice for over fifteen years, both in China and the US. He is the editor and publisher of the largest English-speaking Taoist journal, *The Empty Vessel: A Journal of Taoist Philosophy and Practice*. He leads tours to China to study qigong and visit sacred mountains, and is past president of the National Qigong Association and founding member of the sacred music group Windhorse. He has written a number of successful books on Taoism and qigong.

John Cleare is an internationally renowned photographer specialising in mountains and landscapes. His inspirational and evocative photographs illustrate *Tao Te Ching,* also published by Watkins Publishing.

By the same author

A Gathering of Cranes: Bringing the Tao to the West
Embarking on the Way: A Guide to Western Taoism
The Essence of Qigong (editor)

Tao Paths series:

Good Fortune
Love
Long Life
Harmony

Chi: Energy of Harmony
Chi: Energy of Happiness

Dataclysm

What Our Online Lives Tell Us About Our Offline Selves

Christian Rudder

4th Estate • London

4th Estate
An imprint of HarperCollins*Publishers*
77–85 Fulham Palace Road
London W6 8JB
4thEstate.co.uk

First published in Great Britain by 4th Estate in 2014
This paperback edition published in 2016

1

Grateful acknowledgment is made to *Psychology Today Magazine* for permission to
reprint an excerpt from "Final Analysis: Missed Connections" by Dorothy Gambrell
(January/February 2013), copyright © 2013 by Sussex Publishers, LLC. Reprinted by
permission of Psychology Today Magazine. Image on page 45: Film still from *Dazed and
Confused*, copyright © 1993 by Polygram Filmed Entertainment. Reprinted by permission
of Universal Studios Licensing LLC. Table on page 173: "Zipf's Law and Vocabulary" by
C. J. Sorell from *The Encyclopedia of Applied Linguistics*, edited by C. A. Chapelle
(Oxford: Wiley Blackwell, 2012). Reprinted by permission of the author. Table on page
239: Traits predicted by a Facebook user's "likes" adapted from Figure 2, "Prediction
accuracy of classification of dichotomous/dichotomized attributes expressed by the
AUC" in "Private Traits and Attributes Are Predictable from Digital Records of Human
Behavior" by Michael Kosinskia, David Stillwell, and Thore Graepel (Washington, DC:
PNAS, 2013). Reprinted by permission of the Proceedings of the National Academy
of Sciences of the United States of America.

A catalogue record for this book is available from the British Library

ISBN 978-0-00-749443-9

Original book design by Maria Elias

Printed and bound in Great Britain by Clays Ltd, St Ives plc

MIX
Paper from
responsible sources

FSC™
www.fsc.org

FSC® C007454